Delicious Cupcakes

Delicious Cupcakes

Introduction

Cupcakes

Cupcakes, those elegant little cakes with their luscious toppings, are not only the latest trend to sweep our cafés but they are also stealing the limelight from former stars of the cake world. The unlimited decorating possibilities and foolproof recipes contained in this book are sure to make these small, sweet fancies a huge success.

Compared to muffins, which are less sweet and more rustic in character, cupcakes are elegant, miniature cakes, which are usually made from a smooth cake batter and crowned with sweet buttercream or cream cheese frosting.

Cupcake batter generally contains larger quantities of eggs and sugar and is beaten until very light and creamy. Once the butter or oil, sugar and eggs have been thoroughly blended using an electric hand mixer, the remaining ingredients are

folded in and mixed into a homogenous batter.

Another characteristic feature of cupcakes is the obligatory frosting, which can either be artistically piped on, using a large icing nozzle, or roughly spread over the cupcakes with the aid of a palette knife. Any lavish decoration of your choice can then be added as a finishing touch.

Since cupcakes are luxuriously sweet and creamy, they are an ideal accompaniment to afternoon coffee but are also perfect for serving as an elegant dessert.

Frosting and more —
The icing on the cupcake

Traditional American cupcakes are covered with luscious toppings, many of which are also coloured with food dyes. However, the recipes in this book deliberately avoid relying on food colouring, preferring instead to use puréed fruit, cinnamon or chocolate to colour the frostings. There are, of course, many different food colourings available, suitable for all kinds of occasions, which can be used to brighten up pale buttercream or cream cheese toppings and even the sponge itself. Liquid or paste dyes are recommended to achieve a uniform finish. When deciding on the right amount to use, bear in mind that 'less is often more'. Start by using a small amount of colouring and add more as required. One attractive option is to divide plain sponge batter into four portions and to then colour each portion with a different colour.

Taking a spoonful from each portion at a time, build up layers of the different colours in the cupcake moulds, then finish off the recipe in the usual way. Your guests will be amazed when they eventually take a bite out of their cupcakes!

In addition to the traditional methods of applying frosting to the cooled cupcakes, which include using a rounded knife, palette knife or a piping bag with a large star-shaped nozzle, there is no end to the number of other creative opportunities: a piping bag with a selection of different tips can be used to fashion rose petals, rosettes or a variety of flowers, creating little works of art in the process. Your cupcakes will delight the eye and look almost too good to eat. If the frosting starts to become a little runny, place it in the fridge for a few minutes until it becomes firm again. This will make it much easier to handle.

Depending on the type of frosting used and how much of the surface is covered, the cupcake can be decorated with a whole range of colourful additions, such as coloured sugar beads, chocolate strands, nuts, cracknel, coconut chips, fruits or marzipan – you can let your imagination run riot.

Making and storing cupcakes correctly

Cupcakes are baked in muffin trays. A standard tin will have
12 moulds, each of which should either be greased and dusted
with flour or contain a colourful paper case. Nowadays, extra
small or high-sided moulds are also available as well as the
appropriate paper cases to go with them. If you do not happen
to have a proper muffin baking tray, you can simply use two
paper baking cases, one inside the other, and place these on a
baking tray. Another option is to mould some extra-strong
aluminium foil around the base of a drinking glass to fashion a
baking case. Once baked, cupcakes are suitable for freezing
without their frosting and then, when required, can be baked for
about 10–15 minutes at 180 °C. Any leftover cake mixture can
simply be spooned into paper cases, placed in the depressions
of the muffin tray, and then frozen. It can then be stored in a
freezer bag. When required for use, simply place the uncooked
mixture in the muffin tray and bake according to the recipe
instructions, extending the baking time by approx. 5–10 minutes.
Cupcakes with frosting should be packed in an airtight container
and can be stored for at least 1–2 days in the fridge. They
should be removed from the fridge approx. 30 minutes before
eating so that the frosting has a chance to soften. Any leftover
frosting can be stored in the fridge for several days.

Tips and tricks when making cupcakes

Traditional American cupcakes generally consist of a relatively basic, light sponge batter. The frosting, on the other hand, is therefore often all the more substantial and may consist of double cream cheese or butter with large amounts of icing sugar and additions such as chocolate, vanilla or fresh fruit purées. Below you will find a few tips which you may find useful when making our cupcake recipes:

- Generally speaking, our recipes use vanillin in powder form, which contains real vanilla extract. If so desired, you can obviously also use the scooped out pulp of actual vanilla pods. In this case, the pulp from approx. half a vanilla pod would be enough for each cupcake recipe. Needless to say, the vanilla can also be substituted by vanilla essence in liquid or powdered form or vanilla sugar. Vanilla sugar should not be used for the frosting, however, as it would be too coarse-grained for the smooth cream.

- When making cupcakes, try and use the freshest and least processed products available and take care to ensure that all the ingredients are at room temperature during preparation. As a general rule, butter should be soft so that it can be more easily creamed for the sponge mixture and frosting. Eggs should be removed from the fridge in good time to avoid the possibility of the butter and egg mixture curdling later on. Any cream cheese required for the frosting should also be at room temperature so that it can be whisked to a light and airy consistency with the sifted icing sugar.

- For best results, we recommend using dairy products that are made with whole milk, in other words, yoghurt 3.5 %, milk 3.5 % and double cream cheese. If you want to cut down on calories, it is better to do this by using half-fat butter and low-fat milk for the sponge mix. Low-fat cream cheese, margarine or half-fat butter alternatives are unfortunately not recommended for use in frosting.

- We have tried to ensure that the various sponge and frosting recipes can be mixed and matched wherever possible, thereby providing lots of scope for all kinds of new recipe ideas. Why not experiment with cinnamon frosting on red wine cupcakes, nougat frosting on banana cupcakes or a rich chocolate frosting on vanilla cupcakes? There is no end to the potential diversity of flavours. Even individual ingredients can be easily substituted: for example, pecan nuts can be replaced with walnuts, ground almonds with ground hazelnuts or dark chocolate whole milk chocolate.

We wish you every success and hope you have lots of fun baking, decorating and eating the fruits of your labours!

Recipe section

Blueberry cupcakes with cream

Makes 6 cakes

50 g soft butter
70 g sugar
1 egg
60 g flour
½ tsp baking powder
40 ml milk
80 g blueberries
80 ml cream
2 tsp vanilla sugar

Preheat the oven to 175 °C (or 150 °C if using a fan oven).
Cream the butter and sugar together until light and frothy. Stir
in the egg. Mix the flour and baking powder together, then add
a little at a time to the cake mixture, alternating with the milk.
Wash and pick over the blueberries, then pat dry. Blend half
the berries carefully into the cake batter. Divide the cake
mixture equally between the heart-shaped moulds and bake for
approx. 20 minutes in the centre of the oven. Then, leave to
cool on a wire rack.
Meanwhile, whisk the cream and vanilla sugar until very stiff
before spooning the cream mixture onto the cooled cupcakes
and decorating with the remaining blueberries. Serve
immediately.

Tiramisu cupcakes with espresso

Makes 6 cakes

1 egg
50 g sugar
30 g flour
30 g cornstarch
½ tsp instant vanilla
   pudding powder

½ tsp baking powder
100 g mascarpone
25 g sifted icing sugar
½ cup of strong espresso
40 ml cream
cocoa powder for dusting

Preheat the oven to 175 °C (or 150 °C if using a fan oven). Separate the egg. Whisk the egg white until very stiff. Gradually trickle in the sugar and continue to whisk until the mixture is very stiff and glossy. Add the egg yolk and blend thoroughly.
Combine the flour, cornstarch, vanilla pudding powder and baking powder. Sift into the egg mixture and carefully blend together. Divide the cake batter evenly between the heart-shaped moulds. Bake for approx. 20 minutes on the middle shelf of the oven. Leave to cool for a little while before turning the cakes out onto a wire rack and leaving to cool completely.
Meanwhile, beat the mascarpone cheese and icing sugar together until light and frothy. Stir in 1 tbsp espresso. Whisk the cream until stiff and fold into the mascarpone mixture. Prick the cooled cupcakes several times with a fork. Using a teaspoon, carefully drizzle the remaining espresso over the cupcakes. Then, top the cupcakes with the mascarpone cream and spread evenly using a palette knife. Place in the fridge and dust with cocoa powder before serving.

Black Forest cupcakes

Makes 6 cakes

25 g dark chocolate
  couverture
15 g butter
1 egg
1 pinch salt
1 egg yolk

30 g sugar
50 g flour
½ tsp baking powder
70 ml cream, 2 tsp vanilla sugar
1 cl kirsch
100 g cherry compote
dark chocolate, grated

Preheat the oven to 175 °C (or 150 °C if using a fan oven). Melt the couverture chocolate and butter in a bain-marie, then leave to cool for a short while.

Separate the egg. Whisk the egg white and a pinch of salt together until very stiff. Beat the egg yolks and sugar together until light and frothy. Blend the chocolate and butter mixture with the egg yolks, then carefully fold in the egg white. Combine the flour and baking powder, sift onto the egg mixture and blend together well.

Divide the cake batter between the moulds and bake for about 20 minutes. When baked, press the cupcakes out of their moulds and place on a wire rack to cool completely.

Whisk the cream and vanilla sugar together until stiff. When cool, slice the cupcakes in half horizontally. Drizzle kirsch over the bottom half of each cake and then spoon 2 tsp of cherry compote onto each one and spread lightly. Next, top these bases with 1 tbsp cream before replacing the tops of the cupcakes and pressing down gently. Spread the remaining mascarpone cream on the top of each cupcake. Sprinkle with grated chocolate and refrigerate for 30 minutes before serving.

Strawberry cupcakes with strawberry frosting

Makes 6 cakes

35 g soft butter
50 g sugar
½ tsp vanillin (vanilla powder)
1 egg
80 g flour
½ tsp baking powder
1 pinch salt
20 ml milk
50 g finely chopped
   strawberries

For the frosting:
25 g soft butter
25 g double cream cheese
20 g finely chopped
   strawberries
70 g sifted icing sugar

Preheat the oven to 175 °C (or 150 °C if using a fan oven). Beat the butter, sugar and vanillin together until creamy, then stir in the egg. Combine the flour, baking powder and salt, then take turns mixing first the flour, then the milk into the butter and egg mixture. Finally, stir in the chopped strawberries.
Divide the cake batter equally between the cupcake moulds and bake for approx. 20 minutes on the middle shelf of the oven. Leave to cool on a wire rack.
Meanwhile, to make the frosting, mix all the ingredients together thoroughly until they form a creamy topping. If the frosting is not quite firm enough, stir in a little more icing sugar. Place the frosting in the refrigerator until required, then spoon the mixture into a piping bag fitted with a large nozzle and pipe the frosting onto the cupcakes or smooth it over the surface using a palette knife.

Chocolate chip cupcakes

Makes 6 cakes

30 g soft butter
60 g sugar
1 tsp vanilla sugar
1 egg
60 g flour
½ tsp baking powder
¼ tsp bicarbonate of soda
1 pinch of salt
35 g natural yoghurt

50 g dark chocolate, chopped
coloured sugar beads and strands
  for decoration

For the frosting:
30 g dark chocolate couverture
70 g soft butter
100 g sifted icing sugar

Preheat the oven to 175 °C (or 150 °C if using a fan oven).
Cream the butter, sugar and vanilla sugar together until light
and frothy, then blend in the egg. Combine the flour, baking
powder, bicarbonate of soda and salt, then stir these
ingredients into the butter mixture, a little at a time and
alternating with some of the yoghurt. Blend in the chocolate.
Divide the sponge batter equally between the cake moulds
and bake for approx. 20 minutes in the centre of the oven.
Remove from the oven and cool on a wire rack.
Meanwhile, melt the chocolate for the frosting in a bain-marie
and allow to cool a little. Beat the butter until light and frothy,
add the chocolate and mix together until creamy. Finally, mix in
the icing sugar, making sure it is thoroughly blended. If the
frosting is not quite firm enough, add a little more icing sugar.
Transfer the frosting to a piping bag fitted with a large nozzle
and pipe the topping over the cupcakes. Decorate with sugar
beads and strands.

Caramel cupcakes with caramel topping

Makes 6 cakes

45 g butter
35 g white chocolate
   couverture, chopped
50 g brown sugar
50 ml milk
40 g flour
½ tsp baking powder
1 pinch salt
1 egg

For the topping:
40 g brown sugar
30 g butter
40 ml cream
½ tsp vanillin (vanilla
   powder)

Preheat the oven to 175 °C (or 150 °C if using a fan oven). Melt the butter, white couverture, brown sugar and milk in a small saucepan over a low heat and continue stirring until all the ingredients are uniformly blended. Remove from the heat and leave to cool for approx. 10 minutes.

Combine the flour, baking powder and salt and stir into the caramel mixture, adding the egg last of all. Divide the mixture evenly between the heart-shaped moulds and bake on the middle shelf of the oven for about 30 minutes. Leave to cool in the cake tin.

Meanwhile, melt the ingredients for the topping in a small saucepan, bring to a boil and then simmer gently for about 5 minutes over a low heat. Pour the caramel topping, whilst still warm, over the warm cupcakes and serve.

Pecan cupcakes with cream cheese

Makes 6 cakes

60 g double cream cheese
1 tsp vanilla sugar
70 g sugar, 1 egg
20 g melted butter
40 g flour, 1 tbsp cocoa powder
20 g pecan nuts, coarsely chopped
halved pecan nuts for decorating

For the frosting:
50 g soft butter
1 tbsp milk
40 g sifted icing sugar
1 tbsp cocoa powder

Preheat the oven to 175 °C (or 150 °C if using a fan oven). Beat the cream cheese and vanilla sugar together with 25 g sugar until creamy, then place in the fridge.
Whisk the egg until light and frothy, trickle in the remaining sugar and beat until creamy. Stir in the butter, mix the flour and cocoa powder together, then sift onto the egg mixture. Briefly mix all the ingredients together, then stir in the nuts by hand. Divide half the mixture equally between the cupcake moulds and level off. Spoon about 1 tsp of cream cheese on each one and then cover with the remaining cake batter. Bake the cupcakes in the centre of the oven for about 20 minutes, then cool on a wire rack.
Meanwhile, make the frosting: in a small saucepan, melt the butter in the milk over a low heat, then remove from the hob. Stir in the icing sugar and cocoa powder. If the frosting is still too runny, stir in a little more icing sugar. Once the cupcakes have cooled, spread the frosting over the top and decorate with the halved pecan nuts. Refrigerate until ready to serve.

Coconut cupcakes with cream cheese frosting

Makes 6 cakes

40 g white chocolate couverture
40 g butter
1 egg
40 g sugar
45 g flour
35 g coconut flakes
½ tsp baking powder
40 ml coconut milk

For the frosting:
70 g double cream cheese
40 g icing sugar, sifted
35 g coconut flakes
coconut chips for the
    decoration
cocoa powder for dusting

Preheat the oven to 175 °C (or 150 °C if using a fan oven). Melt the couverture chocolate and butter in a small saucepan over a low heat and then set aside to cool a little.

Separate the egg and whisk the egg white until stiff. Trickle in 25 g sugar and blend until the mixture takes on a firm, glossy consistency.

Beat the egg yolk with the remaining sugar until thick and creamy, then stir in the chocolate and butter mixture.

Combine the flour, coconut flakes and baking powder. Add these ingredients and the coconut milk to the cake batter, alternately stirring in first one, then the other. Finally fold in the beaten egg white.

Divide the cake batter equally between the cupcake moulds and bake in the centre of the oven for approx. 20 minutes. Set aside to cool on a wire rack. Meanwhile, thoroughly blend the frosting ingredients together and spread over the cupcakes using a palette knife. Decorate by sprinkling coconut chips and cocoa powder over the top.

Chocolate cupcakes with chocolate frosting

Makes 6 cakes

45 g butter
50 g sugar
1 tsp vanilla sugar
1 egg
1 tbsp cocoa powder
50 g flour
½ tsp baking powder
¼ tsp bicarbonate of soda
1 pinch of salt

35 g sour cream
white chocolate, grated,
   to decorate

For the frosting:
45 g dark chocolate
   couverture
80 g soft butter
80 g icing sugar, sifted

Preheat the oven to 175 °C (or 150 °C if using a fan oven). In a small saucepan, melt the butter, sugar and vanilla sugar together over a low heat and let cool. Transfer to a mixing bowl and whisk until creamy. Stir in the egg. Dissolve the cocoa powder in approx. 1 tbsp hot water, stir until smooth, then mix into the butter and egg mixture. Combine the flour, baking powder, bicarbonate of soda and salt, then blend into the butter and egg mixture.

Divide the cake batter equally between the cupcake moulds and bake for approx. 20 minutes on the middle shelf of the oven, then set aside to cool.

Meanwhile, prepare the frosting by melting the chocolate in a bain-marie and allowing to cool a little. Transfer the mixture into a piping bag with a large nozzle and pipe the frosting over the cakes to decorate. Finally decorate the surface with a little grated, white chocolate.

Peanut butter cupcakes with cream cheese frosting

Makes 6 cakes

30 g soft butter
20 g peanut butter
50 g brown sugar
½ tsp vanillin (vanilla powder)
½ tsp baking powder
1 egg
50 g flour
a pinch of salt
35 ml buttermilk
peanuts for the decoration

For the frosting:
30 g butter
40 g double cream cheese
50 g icing sugar, sifted
¼ tsp vanillin (vanilla powder)

Preheat the oven to 175 °C (or 150 °C if using a fan oven). Beat the butter and peanut butter together until light and creamy. Mix the sugar and vanillin together, then slowly trickle them into the butter mixture. Mix all the ingredients together until pale and creamy. Add the egg and thoroughly blend into the mixture. Combine the flour, baking powder and salt, then mix into the cake batter, alternately adding small amounts of the dry ingredients and some of the buttermilk.

Divide the mixture equally between the baking moulds and bake on the middle shelf of the oven for approx. 20 minutes. Place on a wire rack and let cool completely.

Meanwhile, prepare the frosting: beat the butter and cream cheese together until creamy, add the icing sugar and vanillin and beat to a smooth consistency. Transfer the frosting into a piping bag fitted with a large nozzle and pipe the topping onto the cupcakes or spread it on using a palette knife. Decorate with peanuts.

Vanilla cupcakes with vanilla frosting

Makes 6 cakes

40 g soft butter
60 g sugar
½ tsp vanillin
1 egg
1 egg yolk
80 g flour
½ tsp baking powder
1 pinch salt
60 ml buttermilk
coloured sugar strands,
   to decorate

For the frosting:
50 g soft butter
50 g icing sugar, sifted
¼ tsp vanillin (vanilla powder)

Preheat the oven to 175 °C (or 150 °C if using a fan oven). Beat the butter, sugar and vanillin together until light and frothy, blend in the egg and egg yolk, adding each one separately. Combine the flour, baking powder and salt and add to the butter mixture, alternately adding small amounts of the flour mixture and buttermilk.

Divide the cake batter equally into the cake moulds and bake for approx. 20 minutes in the centre of the oven. Turn out onto a wire rack and let cool completely.

Meanwhile, prepare the frosting: beat the butter, icing sugar and vanillin together until light and frothy. Transfer the topping into a piping bag fitted with a large nozzle and pipe the frosting onto the cupcakes in a spiral pattern. Sprinkle with sugar strands and serve.

Banana cupcakes with walnuts

Makes 6 cakes

35 g soft butter
50 g brown sugar
1 tsp vanilla sugar
1 egg
50 g flour
½ tsp baking powder
¼ tsp bicarbonate of soda
1 pinch of salt
1 pinch of cinnamon
1 ripe banana

25 ml buttermilk
20 g walnut kernels, roughly
   chopped
6 walnut halves, to decorate

For the frosting:
60 g soft butter
40 g double cream cheese
70 g icing sugar, sifted
½ tsp vanillin (vanilla powder)

Preheat the oven to 175 °C (or 150 °C if using a fan oven).
Cream the butter, sugar and vanilla sugar together and stir in
the egg. Combine the flour, baking powder, bicarbonate of
soda, salt and cinnamon. Mash the banana using a fork and mix
with the buttermilk. Alternately add the flour and banana pulp
to the butter and egg mixture. Finally, stir in the walnuts.
Divide the cupcake batter equally between the baking moulds,
bake for approx. 20 minutes in the centre of the oven, then
leave to cool on a wire rack.
Meanwhile, to make the frosting, beat the butter and cream
cheese together until creamy. Blend in the icing sugar and
vanillin. Spread the cream over the cupcakes using a palette
knife. Decorate each one with half a walnut and serve.

Cupcakes with chocolate cream filling

Makes 6 cakes

1 egg
35 g sugar
1 egg yolk
30 g flour
30 g cornstarch
½ tbsp cocoa powder

½ tsp baking powder
40 g milk chocolate couverture
70 ml crème fraîche
35 ml cream
white chocolate, grated,
   to decorate

Preheat the oven to 175 °C (or 150 °C if using a fan oven). Separate the egg. Beat the egg white until very stiff. Gradually add the sugar to the egg white, a little at a time, and continue to mix until the batter takes on a glossy consistency. Add the egg yolks and mix thoroughly. Combine the flour, cornstarch, cocoa powder and baking powder. Sift the flour mixture onto the eggs and carefully blend in.

Divide the cake batter equally between the cake moulds and bake for 20 minutes in the centre of the oven. Allow to cool for 5 minutes in the baking tin, then tip out onto a wire rack and leave to cool completely.

Melt the chocolate in a bain-marie. Gradually stir in the crème fraîche a little at a time. Place the mixture in the fridge until firm. Whisk the cream until stiff. Beat the thickened chocolate cream with an electric hand mixer until light and frothy, then fold in the whisked cream. Refrigerate until ready to eat.

Slice the cupcakes in half horizontally. Spread one teaspoon of chocolate cream onto the bottom half of each cake, then replace the top half. Place the remaining cream in a piping bag fitted with a large nozzle, then pipe the topping onto the cupcakes. Sprinkle with the grated white chocolate and refrigerate.

Chocolate cherry cupcakes

Makes 6 cakes

100 ml milk
25 g sugar
½ packet of vanilla pudding powder
50 g morello cherries in a jar
85 g soft butter
35 g sugar
1 tsp vanilla sugar

1 pinch of salt
1 egg
1 egg yolk
70 g flour
½ tsp baking powder
½ tbsp cocoa powder
6 cherries for decoration

Preheat the oven to 175 °C (or 150 °C if using a fan oven). Using the milk, sugar and pudding powder, make a set pudding following the instructions on the packet, then leave to cool. Thoroughly drain the cherries in a sieve.

Cream 40 g butter, sugar, vanilla sugar and salt together until very light and frothy. Mix in the egg and egg yolk, one after the other. Mix the flour and baking powder together and add to the butter mixture.

Divide half the cake batter equally between the heart-shaped moulds. Add the cocoa powder to the remaining cake mixture and mix well. Divide the dark cake batter between the cake moulds in the same way. Gently press 2 cherries into the cake batter in each mould. Bake the cupcakes for about 20 minutes in the centre of the oven. Turn out onto a wire rack and let cool completely.

Meanwhile, beat the remaining butter until light and creamy, then blend in the cooled, set pudding a little at a time until the mixture forms a homogenous buttercream. Transfer the cream to a piping bag fitted with a large nozzle and spread evenly over the cupcakes. Finally, top each cupcake with a cherry.

Vanilla and almond cupcakes

Makes 6 cakes

1 egg
35 g sugar
1 tsp vanilla sugar
50 g flour
½ tsp baking powder
flaked almonds, to decorate
butter and ground almonds for the baking tray

For the cream:
130 ml cream
⅓ sachet of instant vanilla cream powder

Preheat the oven to 170 °C (or 150 °C if using a fan oven).
Grease the baking moulds and sprinkle with ground almonds.
Beat the egg until frothy and creamy, then trickle in the sugar
and vanilla sugar and continue beating all the ingredients
together until creamy. Combine the flour and baking powder,
sift into the egg mixture and mix briefly by hand.
Divide the cake batter between the heart-shaped moulds and
bake on the middle shelf of the oven for about 20 minutes.
Tip out onto a wire rack and leave to cool.
To make the cream topping, whisk the cream and vanilla cream
powder together until stiff. Slice the cupcakes in half horizontally,
spread the bottom half of each one with 1–2 tsp of the cream
and then replace each top half. Transfer the remaining cream
into a piping bag fitted with a large nozzle and pipe over the
cupcakes. Toast the almonds in a dry frying pan, sprinkle over
the cupcakes and then refrigerate until ready to serve.

Apple and cinnamon cupcakes with cinnamon frosting

Makes 6 cakes

40 g soft butter
40 g sugar
1 egg
50 g flour
½ tsp cinnamon
½ tsp baking powder
1 apple
apple slices, to decorate

For the frosting:
50 g double cream cheese
30 g soft butter
½ tsp cinnamon
100 g icing powder, sifted

Preheat the oven to 170 °C (or 150 °C if using a fan oven). Beat the butter and sugar together until creamy, then stir in the egg. Combine the flour with the cinnamon and baking powder and mix into the butter and egg mixture.

Peel, quarter and core the apple, then either chop the fruit into small pieces or grate, as desired. Stir the apple into the cake batter, then divide it equally between the baking moulds and bake in the centre of the oven for about 25 minutes. Place the cakes on a wire rack to cool thoroughly.

To make the frosting, beat the cream cheese and butter together until creamy. Mix the cinnamon and icing sugar together, before blending them into the cream cheese and butter. If the consistency is too runny, stir in a little more icing sugar. Transfer the frosting into a piping bag fitted with a large nozzle and squeeze over the cupcakes. Decorate with a few thin slices of apple.

Chocolate cupcakes with sour cream frosting

Makes 6 cakes

40 g soft butter
50 g sugar
1 tsp vanilla sugar
1 egg
50 g flour
¼ tsp baking powder
1 pinch salt
35 g dark chocolate
35 g sour cream
grated chocolate, to decorate

For the frosting:
50 g soft butter
1 tbsp sour cream
½ tsp vanillin (vanilla powder)
70 g icing sugar, sifted

Preheat the oven to 170 °C (or 150 °C if using a fan oven). Beat the butter, sugar and vanilla sugar together until creamy, then stir in the egg. Combine the flour, baking powder and salt and stir into the butter and egg mixture.

Melt the chocolate in a bain-marie, allow to cool slightly, then stir into the cake batter, stirring constantly. Finally, blend in the sour cream.

Divide the mixture between the baking moulds, bake for about 20 minutes in the centre of the oven, then leave to cool on a wire rack.

To make the frosting, cream the butter, sour cream and vanillin together until light and frothy, then stir in the icing sugar. If the frosting is too runny, stir in a little more icing sugar until the desired consistency is reached. Transfer the frosting to an icing bag fitted with a large nozzle and pipe onto the cupcakes or spread over the surface with a palette knife. Sprinkle the cupcakes with grated chocolate before serving.

Egg liqueur cupcakes with egg liqueur topping

Makes 6 cakes

1 egg
1 egg yolk
50 g sugar
1 tsp vanilla sugar
35 ml vegetable oil
35 ml egg liqueur
80 g flour
½ tsp baking powder

For the topping:
55 g icing sugar, sifted
2 tbsp egg liqueur

Preheat the oven to 170 °C (or 150 °C if using a fan oven). Beat the eggs, sugar and vanilla sugar together until creamy, then stir in the oil and egg liqueur. Mix the flour and baking powder together, then stir into the egg and oil mixture.

Divide the cake mixture between the baking moulds and bake in the centre of the oven for about 20 minutes. Leave to cool on a wire rack.

To make the topping, blend the icing sugar and egg liqueur to a smooth paste. If the topping is too runny, stir in additional icing sugar. Spread over the cupcakes and leave to set.

Hazelnut cupcakes with hazelnut frosting

Makes 6 cakes

35 g soft butter
40 g sugar
1 egg
50 g flour
½ tbsp cocoa powder
½ tsp baking powder
35 g hazelnut spread
hazelnut cracknel, to decorate

For the frosting:
30 g soft butter
100 g icing sugar, sifted
30 g hazelnut spread

Preheat the oven to 170 °C (or 150 °C if using a fan oven). Beat the butter and sugar together until creamy, then stir in the egg. Mix the flour, cocoa powder and baking powder together and stir into the butter and egg mixture. Finally, blend in the hazelnut spread.

Divide the cake mixture between the baking moulds and bake on the middle shelf of the oven for about 20 minutes. Leave the cakes to cool on a wire rack.

Meanwhile, to make the frosting, beat the butter and icing sugar together until very creamy, then mix in the hazelnut spread. If the mixture is too runny, stir in a little more icing sugar. Transfer the frosting to a piping bag fitted with a large nozzle and squeeze the topping over the cupcakes or spread it over the surface using a palette knife. Sprinkle with hazelnut cracknel.

Chocolate cupcakes with espresso buttercream

Makes 6 cakes

20 g butter
30 g brown sugar
1 tsp vanilla sugar
1 egg
90 g flour
½ tbsp cocoa powder
½ tsp baking powder
1 pinch of salt
20 g sour cream
20 ml freshly brewed espresso

1 tsp instant espresso powder
6 coffee beans, to decorate

For the buttercream:
1 egg white
25 g sugar
1 tsp vanilla sugar
35 g soft butter
½ tsp instant espresso powder

Preheat the oven to 170 °C (or 150 °C if using a fan oven). Beat the butter, sugar and vanilla sugar together until creamy, then stir in the egg. Combine the flour, cocoa powder, baking powder and salt, then gradually add alternate amounts of the flour mixture and sour cream to the butter and egg mixture. Mix the cooled espresso and instant espresso powder together, then stir into the cake batter.

Divide the cake batter between the baking moulds and bake in the centre of the oven for about 20 minutes. Turn out onto a wire rack and leave to cool.

Meanwhile, to make the buttercream, lightly whisk the egg white in a bowl over a warm bain-marie using a hand whisk. Trickle in the sugar and vanilla sugar and keep stirring constantly until all the sugar is dissolved. Do not let the mixture become too hot or the egg white will begin to solidify. Transfer to a large mixing bowl and whisk for several minutes to produce a light, fluffy consistency which forms stiff peaks.

Add small amounts of butter to the egg white, stirring constantly, and continue to whisk for several more minutes. Finally, stir in the instant espresso powder. Top the cupcakes with the buttercream, shaping it into a peak. Decorate each peak with a coffee bean.

Orangeade cupcakes with sour cream topping

Makes 6 cakes

1 egg
35 g sugar
1 tsp vanilla sugar
20 ml vegetable oil
50 g flour
¼ tsp baking powder
20 ml orangeade
coloured sugar strands,
   to decorate

For the sour cream topping:
70 ml cream
1 tsp vanilla sugar
50 g sour cream
½ packet of vanilla sauce
   powder (instant)

Preheat the oven to 170 °C (or 150 °C if using a fan oven). Beat the egg, sugar and vanilla sugar together until creamy, then blend in the oil. Mix the flour and baking powder together, then mix alternate amounts of flour and orangeade into the butter and egg mixture. Divide the cake batter between the baking moulds and bake for about 20 minutes on the middle shelf of the oven. Turn out onto a wire rack and leave to cool. To make the sour cream topping, whisk the cream and vanilla sugar together until stiff, then blend in the sour cream and vanilla sauce powder until the mixture is light but forms firm peaks. Spread this over the cupcakes using a palette knife. Sprinkle with coloured sugar strands.

Marble cupcakes with whipped cream

Makes 6 cakes

35 g soft butter
50 g sugar
1 egg
1 egg yolk
60 g flour
½ tsp baking powder
120 ml cream
½ tbsp cocoa powder
2 tsp vanilla sugar
cocoa powder, for dusting

Preheat the oven to 170 °C (or 150 °C if using a fan oven).
Cream the butter and sugar together, then stir in the egg and
egg yolk, separately. Mix the flour and baking powder together,
then add the flour and 30 ml of cream, alternately, to the butter
and egg mixture.
Using half the cake batter, divide it between the baking
moulds. Stir the cocoa powder into the other half of the cake
mixture. Layer the dark cake batter on top of the plain mixture.
Draw a fork through the mixture from the bottom to the top to
create a marbling effect. Bake for approx. 20 minutes in the
centre of the oven. Place the cakes on a wire rack and let cool.
Whisk the remaining cream and vanilla sugar together until stiff.
Dust with a little cocoa powder and serve.

Raspberry yoghurt cupcakes

Makes 6 cakes

1 egg
50 g sugar
1 tsp vanilla sugar
35 ml vegetable oil
35 g natural yoghurt
70 g flour
½ tsp baking powder
50 g raspberries, frozen
6 fresh raspberries, to
  decorate

For the frosting:
20 g soft butter
20 g double cream cheese
20 g fresh raspberries, finely
  chopped and sifted
100 g icing sugar, sifted

Preheat the oven to 170 °C (or 150 °C if using a fan oven). Beat the egg, sugar and vanilla sugar until creamy, then stir in the oil and yoghurt. Combine the flour and baking powder and stir into the sponge batter.

Divide the cake mixture between the baking moulds, gently press a few frozen raspberries into the mixture and bake the cupcakes in the centre of the oven for about 20 minutes. Turn out onto a wire rack and leave to cool.

Meanwhile, to make the frosting, thoroughly mix all the ingredients together until creamy. If the frosting is too runny, stir in a little more icing sugar. Place the frosting in the fridge until required. Finally, transfer the frosting to an icing bag with a large star-shaped tip and pipe onto the cupcakes. Decorate with fresh raspberries.

Red wine cupcakes with chocolate frosting

Makes 6 cakes

45 g soft butter
45 g sugar
1 tsp vanilla sugar
1 egg
65 g flour
½ tbsp cocoa powder
½ tsp baking powder
¼ tsp cinnamon
50 ml red wine
25 g dark chocolate, chopped

For the frosting:
40 g dark chocolate
65 g soft butter
80 g icing sugar, sifted

Preheat the oven to 170 °C (or 150 °C if using a fan oven).
Cream the butter, sugar and vanilla sugar together, then blend
in the egg. Combine the flour, cocoa powder, baking powder
and cinnamon, then, alternately, add the dry ingredients and
the red wine to the egg and butter mixture. Finally, add the
chocolate.
Divide the mixture between the baking moulds and bake for
approx. 20 minutes on the middle shelf of the oven. Turn out
onto a wire rack and let cool.
Meanwhile, to make the frosting, melt the chocolate in a bain-
marie before setting aside to cool a little. Cream the butter,
pour in the chocolate and blend until creamy. Finally, add the
icing sugar and mix well. If the frosting is too runny, add a little
more icing sugar. Finally, transfer the topping to an icing bag
fitted with a large nozzle and pipe onto the cupcakes to
decorate.

Maple syrup cupcakes with walnuts

Makes 6 cakes

30 g soft butter
20 g brown sugar
1 tsp vanilla sugar
20 ml maple syrup
1 egg
50 g flour
½ tsp baking powder
1 pinch salt
1 tbsp milk

20 g walnut kernels,
  chopped
6 walnut halves, to decorate

For the frosting:
35 g double cream cheese
30 g soft butter
100 g icing sugar, sifted
1 tbsp maple syrup

Preheat the oven to 170 °C (or 150 °C if using a fan oven). Beat the butter, sugar and vanilla sugar together until creamy. Blend in the maple syrup and mix in the egg. Combine the flour, baking powder and salt and, alternately, mix the dry ingredients and the milk into the butter and egg mixture. Finally, stir in the chopped walnut kernels.

Divide the sponge batter between the baking moulds and bake in the centre of the oven for approx. 20 minutes. Then, turn the cakes out onto a wire rack and allow to cool.

Meanwhile, to make the frosting, cream the butter and cream cheese together, then mix with the icing sugar to form a smooth paste. Finally, blend in the maple syrup. If the frosting is too runny, add a little more icing sugar until the mixture reaches the desired consistency. Transfer the frosting into an icing bag with a nozzle and pipe the topping onto the cupcakes. Decorate with walnut halves.

Vanilla cupcakes with whipped cream

Makes 6 cakes

45 g soft butter
40 g sugar
½ tsp vanillin (vanilla powder)
1 egg
60 g flour
½ tsp baking powder
1 pinch of salt

40 ml buttermilk
35 g strawberry jam
70 ml cream
2 tsp vanilla sugar
6 strawberries, freshly
    washed, to decorate

Preheat the oven to 170 °C (or 150 °C if using the oven). Beat the butter, sugar and vanillin until creamy, then thoroughly blend in the egg. Combine the flour, baking powder and salt and alternately mix the flour and buttermilk into the butter and egg mixture.
Divide half the cupcake batter between the baking moulds. Drop one teaspoon of strawberry jam onto the mixture in each mould, then, top each one with the remaining cake batter. Bake in the centre of the oven for approx. 20 minutes. Turn the cakes out onto a wire rack and leave to cool.
Using a spoon, transfer the whipped cream onto the cooled cupcakes, decorate with a strawberry and serve immediately.